Power Packaging

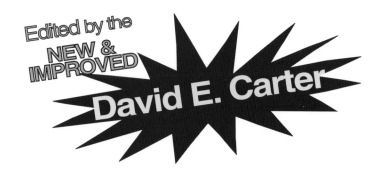

Edited by the
NEW &
IMPROVED
David E. Carter

Book Design
Suzanna M.W. Brown

Production & Layout
Kristin J. Back

Watkins College
of Art & Design

D1205212

Power Packaging

First published 1999 by Hearst Books International
1350 Avenue of the Americas
New York, NY 10019

ISBN: 0688-16817-5

Distributed in the U.S. and Canada by
Watson-Guptill Publications
1515 Broadway
New York, NY 10036
Tel: (800) 451-1741
          (732) 363-4511 in NJ, AK, HI
Fax: (732) 363-0338

ISBN: 0-8230-4261-8

Distributed throughout the rest of the world by
Hearst Books International
1350 Avenue of the Americas
New York, NY 10019
Fax: (212) 261-6795

First Published in Germany by
Nippan
Nippon Shuppan Ilanbai
Deutschland GmbH
D-40549 Dusseldorf
Telephone: (0211) 504 8089
Fax: (0211) 504 9326

ISBN: 3-931884-49-X

Printed in Hong Kong by Everbest Printing Company
through Four Colour Imports, Louisville, Kentucky.

You're about to see some of the best package designs in the world.

The work included in this book includes material which was submitted for two annuals which I edit: *American Corporate Identity* and *The Creativity Annual,* as well as designs which were submitted by some of the top graphic designers from around the world in response to invitations we sent to selected firms.

Inside, you'll see unique solutions to marketing problems, as well as strong executions of corporate identity into a product package.

Package design is one category of corporate identity that is constantly evolving as firms use package updates to freshen brands and to respond to competitive attacks. It is indicative of the rapidly changing nature of this field that many of the designs shown in the book are not for new products, but are package refinements of existing products. Often, a package redesign is the result of a product repositioning or a new market strategy.

As you look at each of the designs included inside, remember that nothing was done just to "look pretty". Packaging is indeed a tool of marketing management, and everything inside this book shows a visual execution of corporate strategies.

My thanks to all the firms who submitted work for this book.

David E. Carter

Table of Contents

design firm: **Klim Design Inc.**
Avon, Connecticut
client: Casa Cuervo S.A. de C.U.

design firm: **Tharp Did It**
Los Gatos, California
designer: Rick Tharp
client: Sebastiani Vineyards

design firm: **Gianninoto Associates**
New York, New York
designers: Gianninoto Associates
client: Grants of Ireland
(*Irish Mist Liquer*)

design firm: **Nolin Larosee Design Communications Inc.**
Montreal, Canada
art director: Marthe Courchesne
client: Société Des Alcools Du Québec

design firm: **Cato Design Inc.**
Richmond, Australia
designers: Cato Design Inc.
client: Peerick

design firm: **Cato Design Inc.**
Richmond, Australia
designers: Cato Design Inc.
client: Rosemount

design firm: **Cato Design Inc.**
Richmond, Australia
designers: Cato Design Inc.
client: T'Gallant

design firm: **Design Core Pty. Ltd.**
                Adelaide, Australia
designer: Elizabeth Schlooz
production: Sergio Jeloscek
photographer: Adam Bruzzone
client: Dalton Fine Paper
                (*Christmas Port 1995*)

design firm: **Cato Design Inc.**
                Richmond, Australia
designers: Cato Design Inc.
client: T'Gallant

design firm: **Mires Design, Inc**
                San Diego, California
art director: José A. Serrano
designer: Miguel Perez
illustrator: Tracy Sabin
client: Bordeaux Printers

7

design firm: **Klim Design Inc.**
               Avon, Connecticut
\client: Casa Cuervo S.A. de C.U.

design firm: **Blackburn's Ltd.**
               London, England
creative director:
               John Blackburn
art director: Belinda Duggan
illustrator: James Marsh
designers: Roberta Oates, Belinda Duggan
client: Sociedade Dos Vinhos Borges

design firm: **Blackburn's Ltd.**
               London, England
designers: John Blackburn, Belinda Duggan
client: Allied Domecq

design firm: **CDT Design**
               London, England
designers: Mike Dempsey,
               Neil Walker, Susen Vural
client: Seresin Estate

design firm: **Cato Design Inc.**
               Richmond, Australia
designers: Cato Design Inc.
client: T'Gallant

design firm: **Kollberg/Johnson**
New York, New York
designers: Gary Kollberg
Kollberg/Johnson
client: Austin Nichols

design firm: **Elmwood**
Leeds, England
designer: Martyn Hayes
client: Vaux Breweries Ltd.

design firm: **Kollberg/Johnson**
New York, New York
designers: Kollberg/Johnson
client: Austin Nichols

design firm: **Greteman Group**
Wichita, Kansas
creative director:
Sonia Greteman
art directors: Sonia Greteman, James Strange
designers: Sonia Greteman, James Strange, Craig Tomson
client: Tabacos Gran Columbia

design firm: **Blackburn's Ltd.**
London, England
designer: John Blackburn
client: United Distillers & Vintners

design firm: **Curtis Design**
San Francisco, California
designers: Dave Curtis, Sean McGrath
client: Casa Rockefeller S.A.de.C.V.

design firm: **Michael Osborne Design**
San Francisco, California
art director: Michael Osborne
designers: Michael Osborne Design
client: Brown-Forman
Beverages Worldwide

design firm: **Blackburn's Ltd**
London, England
designer: John Blackburn
client: Orchid Drinks

design firm: **SBG Enterprise**
San Francisco, California
designer: Thomas Bond
client: Brown Forman

design firm: **Bailey Design Group, Inc.**
Plymouth Meeting, Pennsylvania
designers: Ken Cahill, Jeff Kowal
client: Paddington Corporation
(*Goldschlager*)

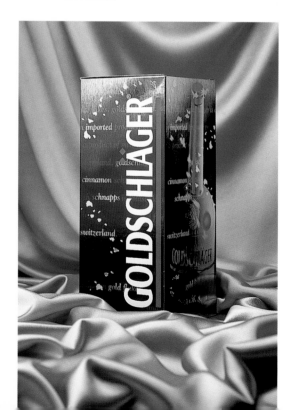

12

design firm: **K–Design**
Escholzmatt, Switzerland
designer: Käthi Friedli-Studer
client: Distillerie Studer & Co AG Escholzmatt

design firm: **Michael Osborne Design**
San Francisco, California
art director: Michael Osborne
designers: Michael Osborne Design
client: Brown-Forman Beverages Worldwide

design firm: **Michael Osborne Design**
San Francisco, California
art director: Michael Osborne
designers: Michael Osborne, Michelle Gottlieb
client: Silver Oaks Cellars

design firm: **Michael Osborne Design**
San Francisco, California
art director: Michael Osborne
designers: Michael Osborne Design
client: Tayland Cellars

design firm: **K-Design**
Escholzmatt, Switzerland
designer: Käthi Friedli-Studer
client: Distillerie Studer & Co AG Escholzmatt

design firm: **Kan & Lau Design Consultants**
Hong Kong, Republic of China
creative director:
Kan Tai-Keung
art directors: Kan Tai-Keung, Chon So Hing
designers: Kan Tai-Keung, Chon So Hing,
Stephen Lau Yu Cheong
client: Bacardi-Martini Asia Pacific Ltd.
(*Commemorative Pack for 1997 Hong Kong*)

design firm: **Haase & Knels, Atelier for design**
Bremen, Germany
creative director:
Sibylle Haase
designer: Katja Hirschfelder
client: Stanwell, tobacco
(*Castello gentile*)

design firm: **Haase & Knels**
Bremen, Germany
creative director:
Sibylle Haase
designer: Katja Hirschfelder
client: Stanwell
(*Edition 96*)

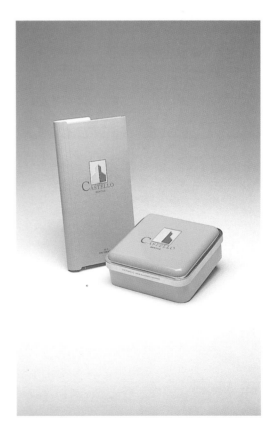

16

design firm: **Praxis Diseñadores Y Asoc., SC**
Mexico, D.F.
art director, designer:
Nadya Villegas
client: Valle Redondo
(*Don Angel Wine*)

design firm: **Haase & Knels, Atelier for design**
Bremen, Germany
creative director:
Harald Schweers
art director: Martina Lüllich
client: Stanwell, tobacco
(*Hacienda*)

design firm: **Haase & Knels, Atelier for design**
Bremen, Germany
creative director:
Sibylle Haase
designer: Katja Hirschfelder
client: Stanwell, tobacco
(*Edition*)

17

design firm: **Elmwood**
                Leeds, England
designer: Andrew Lawrence
client: Asda Stores Ltd.

design firm: **Cato Design Inc.**
                Richmond, Australia
designers: Cato Design Inc.
client: Foster's

design firm: **Turner Duckworth**
                San Francisco, California
designer: David Turner
client: McKenzie River Corp.

design firm: **Cato Design Inc.**
Richmond, Australia
designers: Cato Design Inc.
client: Bond Brewery

design firm: **Blackburn's Ltd.**
London, England
designer: Tom Sutherland
client: Highland Distilleries

design firm: **Bailey Design Group, Inc.**
Plymouth Meeting, Pennsylvania
designers: Dave Fiedler, Wendy Seldomridge
client: Paddington Corporation
(*Puccino*)

design firm: **Curtis Design**
San Francisco, California
designers: Dave Curtis, Chris Benitez
client: Vinomex S.A. de C.V.

design firm: **Blackburn's Ltd.**
London, England
designer: John Blackburn
client: Cockburns Smithes & Co.

design firm: **Blackburn's Ltd.**
London, England
designer: Belinda Duggan
client: Berry Brothers & Rudd

design firm: **K-Design**
Escholzmatt, Switzerland
designer: Käthi Friedli-Studer
client: Distillerie Studer & Co AG Escholzmatt

design firm: **Kollberg/Johnson**
New York, New York
designer: Penny Johnson
client: Jos. E. Seagram

design firm: **Studio Bustamante**
San Diego, California
designer: Gerald Bustamante
client: Kendall Jackson

design firm: **Elmwood**
Leeds, England
designer: Martyn Hayes
client: Asda Stores Ltd.

design firm: **Tharp Did It**
Los Gatos, California
designers: Rick Tharp, Charles Drummond,
Steve Lyons (for Beeline Group)
client: Hiram Walker

design firm: **Colonna Farrell Design**
St. Helena, California
designer: Cynthia Sterling
client: Domaine Chando

design firm: **Kollberg/Johnson**
New York, New York
designer: Penny Johnson
client: Jos. E. Seagram

design firm: **Cato Design Inc.**
Richmond, Australia
designers: Cato Design Inc.
client: Cascade

design firm: **Covey Porter Bell**
London, England
designers: Simon Adamson, Allison Miguel
client: Scottish Courage

design firm: **Landor Associates**
London, England
designers: Landor Associates
client: Danone Group
(*Kronenbourg*)

design firm: **LMS Design**
Stamford, Connecticut
designer: Richard Shear
client: Joseph Victori Inc.

design firm: **Turner Duckworth**
San Francisco, California
designer: David Turner
client: McKenzie River Corp.

design firm: **Sibley Peteet Design**
Dallas, Texas
designers: Tom Hough, David Beck
client: Gambrinus
(*Shiner*)

design firm: **Michael Osborne Design**
San Francisco, California
designers: Michael Osborne Design
art director: Michael Osborne
client: Montevina
(*Sutter Home*)

design firm: **Colonna Farrell Design**
St. Helena, California
designers: Cynthia Sterling, Amy Racina
client: Clos Du Bois

design firm: **Michael Osborne Design**
San Francisco, California
art director: Michael Osborne
designers: Michael Osborne Design
client: Montevina
(*Sutter Home*)

design firm: **Michael Osborne Design**
San Francisco, California
art director: Michael Osborne
designer: Karen Schmucker
client: Barbour Winery

design firm: **Hornall Anderson Design Works, Inc.**
Seattle, Washington
designers: Jack Anderson, Larry Anderson,
Bruce Branson Meyer
client: Rhino Chasers

design firm: **Blackburn's Ltd**
London, England
creative/art director:
John Blackburn
illustrator: Sarah Roberts
designers: Matt Thompson, Sarah Roberts
client: Allied Domecq Spirits & Wine
(*Courvoisier Vs Cognac*)

design firm: **Pearlfisher**
London, England
creative director:
Jonathan Ford
designers: Jonathan Ford, Kate Barsby
client: Seagram
(*Sundsvall*)

design firm: **K-Design**
Escholzmatt, Switzerland
designer: Käthi Friedli-Studer
client: Distillerie Studer & Co AG Escholzmatt

design firm: **Elmwood**
Leeds, England
designer: Karen Ellis
client: Asda Stores Ltd.

design firm: **Pearlfisher**
London, England
creative director:
Jonathan Ford
designers: Jonathan Ford, Andy Willingham
client: Seagram
(*Chivas de Danu*)

design firm: **Elmwood**
Leeds, England
designer: Andrew Lawrence
client: Vaux Breweries Ltd.

design firm: **Mike Salisbury Communications**
Marina Del Rey, California
designer: Mike Salisbury

design firm: **Turner Duckworth**
San Francisco, California
designer: Bruce Duckworth
client: Prospect Beverages

design firm: **Elmwood**
Leeds, England
designer: James Backhurst
client: Vaux Breweries Ltd.

design firm: **Cato Design Inc.**
Richmond, Australia
designers: Cato Design Inc.
client: T'Gallant

design firm: **Blackburn's Ltd.**
London, England
designer: John Blackburn
client: United Distillers & Vintners

design firm: **Studio Bustamante**
San Diego, California
designer: Gerald Bustamante
client: Killians Red

design firm: **K-Design**
Escholzmatt, Switzerland
designer: Käthi Friedli-Studer
client: Distillerie Studer & Co AG Escholzmatt

design firm: **Blackburn's Ltd.**
London, England
designer: Belinda Duggan
client: Berry Brothers & Rudd

design firm: **K-Design**
Escholzmatt, Switzerland
designer: Käthi Friedli-Studer
client: Distillerie Studer & Co AG Escholzmatt

design firm: **Klim Design Inc.**
Avon, Connecticut
client: Casa Cuervo S.A. de C.U.

design firm: **Colonna Farrell Design**
St. Helena, California
client: Domaine Chandon

design firm: **Cato Design Inc.**
Richmond, Australia
designers: Cato Design Inc.
client: T'Gallant

design firm: **Michael Osborne Design**
San Francisco, California
art director: Michael Osborne
designers: Michael Osborne, Michelle Gottlieb
client: Silver Oak Cellars

design firm: **Colonna Farrell Design**
St. Helena, California
designer: Ralph Colonna
client: Jordan Vineyard & Winery

design firm: **Klim Design Inc.**
Avon Connecticut
designer: Matt Klim
client: Casa Cuervo S.A. de C.U.

design firm: **Colonna Farrell Design**
St. Helena, California
designer: Christina Baldwin
client: Grace Family Vineyards

design firm: **Colonna Farrell Design**
St. Helena, California
designers: Cynthia Sterling, Amy Linn
client: Bacio Divino

design firm: **Mark Oliver, Inc.**
Santa Barbara, California
designer: Mark Oliver
client: Firestone Reserve

design firm: **Watts Graphic Design**
South Melbourne, Australia
designers: Helen Watts, Peter Watts
client: Pond Cottage
(*Pond Cottage Port*)

design firm: **Cahan & Associates**
San Francisco, California
designer: Kevin Roberson
client: Apollo Ale

design firm: **Watts Graphic Design**
South Melbourne, Australia
designers: Helen Watts, Peter Watts
client: Watts Graphic Design
(*Watts Christmas Port*)

design firm: **Blackburn's Ltd.**
London, England
designers: John Blackburn, Belinda Duggan
client: Hermann Kendermann/Carl Reh

design firm: **Design Core Pty. Ltd.**
Adelaide, Australia
designer: Elizabeth Schlooz
production: Sergio Jeloscek
photographer: Adam Bruzzone
client: Dalton Fine Paper

design firm: **Hornall Anderson Design Works, Inc.**
               Seattle, Washington
designers: John Hornall, Jana Nishi, Debra McCloskey
client: Gordon Brothers Winery

design firm: **Pearlfisher**
               London, England
designers: Jonathan Ford,
               Karen Welman,
               Kate Barsby
client: Campbell Distillers
               (*House of Lords*)

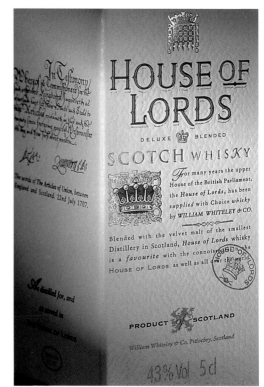

design firm: **Gianninoto Associates**
               New York, New York
designers: Gianninoto Associates
client: Grants of Ireland
               (*Irish Mist Liquer*)

design firm: **Cato Design Inc.**
               Richmond, Australia
designers: Cato Design Inc.
client: Osborns

design firm: **K-Design**
               Escholzmatt, Switzerland
designer: Käthi Friedli-Studer
client: Distillerie Studer & Co AG Escholzmatt

design firm: **Michael Osborne Design**
                San Francisco, California
art director: Michael Osborne
designer: Paul Kagiwada
client: Tayland Cellars

design firm: **Michael Osborne Design**
                San Francisco, California
art director: Michael Osborne
designers: Michael Osborne Design
client: Michael Osborne Design

design firm: **Hans Flink Design Inc.**
                New York, New York
designers: Harry Bertschmann, Hans D. Flink
client: Thiebaud & Co.
                (*Kiss of New York*)

design firm: **Michael Osborne Design**
San Francisco, California
art director: Michael Osborne
designers: Michael Osborne Design
client: Mumm Cuvée Napa

design firm: **Mark Oliver, Inc.**
Santa Barbara, California
designer: Mark Oliver
client: Curtis Winery

design firm: **Cato Design Inc.**
Richmond, Australia
designers: Cato Design, Inc.
client: T'Gallant

design firm: **Sayles Graphic Design**
Des Moines, Iowa
designer: John Sayles
client: Gianna Rose
(*French Soap Cubes*)

design firm: **SBG Enterprise**
San Francisco, California
designer: Mary Brucken
client: Bare Essentials

design firm: **Michael Osborne Design**
San Francisco, California
art director: Michael Osborne
designers: Michael Osborne Design
client: Nordstrom

design firm: **SBG Enterprise**
San Francisco, California
designer: Amy Knapp
client: Bare Essentials

design firm: **SBG Enterprise**
San Francisco, California
designer: Amy Knapp
client: Bare Essentials

design firm: **Sayles Graphic Design**
Des Moines, Iowa
designer: John Sayles
client: Gianna Rose
(*Palm Balm*)

45

design firm: **Hans Flink Design Inc.**
New York, New York
designers: Susan Kunschaft,
Mark Krukonis,
Chang Mei Lin
client: Helene Curtis
(*Rave*)

design firm: **Cato Design Inc.**
Richmond, Australia
designers: Cato Design Inc.
client: Poppy

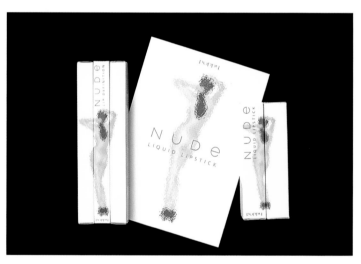

design firm: **Paragon Design International**
Chicago, Illinois
project director:
John Racila
client: Alberto-Culver Co.

46

design firm: **Tom Fowler, Inc.**
                Stamford, Connecticut
designer: Elizabeth P. Ball
client: Chesebrough-Pond's USA Co.

design firm: **Tom Fowler, Inc.**
                Stamford, Connecticut
designers: Thomas G. Fowler,
                Elizabeth P. Ball
client: Chesebrough-Pond's USA Co.

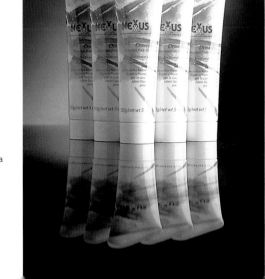

design firm: **Mark Oliver, Inc.**
                Santa Barbara, California
designer: Mark Oliver
client: Nexxus Body Lotion

47

design firm: **Cato Design Inc.**
Richmond, Australia
designers: Cato Design Inc.
client: C'est la Vie

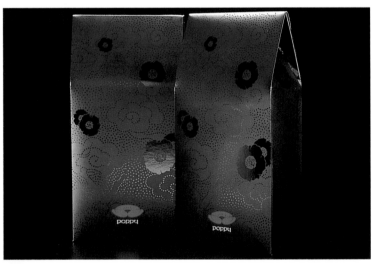

design firm: **Cato Design Inc.**
Richmond, Australia
designers: Cato Design Inc.
client: Poppy

design firm: **Cato Design Inc.**
Richmond, Australia
designers: Cato Design Inc.
client: Coles

design firm: **Cato Design Inc.**
                Richmond, Australia
designers: Cato Design Inc.
client: Poppy

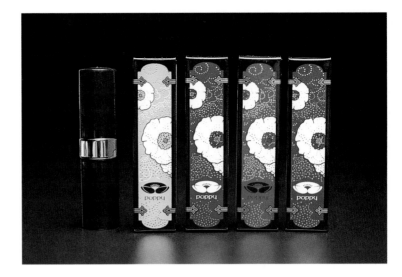

design firm: **Cato Design Inc.**
                Richmond, Australia
designers: Cato Design Inc.
client: Poppy

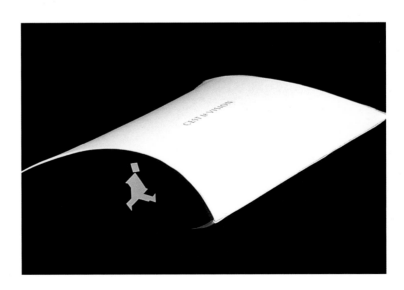

design firm: **Cato Design Inc.**
                Richmond, Australia
designers: Cato Design Inc.
client: C'est la Vie

49

design firm: **Hans Flink Design Inc.**
New York, New York
designers: Harry Bertschmann, Hans D. Flink
client: Chesebrough Pond's
(*Royall Mens Lotions*)

design firm: **Michael Osborne Design**
San Francisco, California
designers: Michael Osborne Design
client: Nordstrom

design firm: **Michael Osborne Design**
San Francisco, California
designers: Michael Osborne Design
client: Nordstrom

design firm: **Oden Marketing & Design**
Memphis, Tennessee
designers: Jill Broadhacker, Bret Terwilleger
creative director:
Bret Terwilleger
client: Yardley

design firm: **SBG Enterprise**
San Francisco, California
designer: Amy Knapp
client: Bare Essentials

design firm: **Covey Porter Design**
London, England
designer: Simon Adamson
client: Charles Worthington

design firm: **Mike Salisbury Communications**
Marina Del Rey, California
designer: Mike Salisbury

design firm: **Pearlfisher**
London, England
designer: Karen Welman
client: Pearlfisher
(*Blue Fragrance*)

design firm: **Advertising Department,**
Leo Pharmaceutical Products
Ballerup, Denmark
designer: Vibeke Nødskov
client: MEKU

design firm: **Hans Flink Design Inc.**
New York, New York
designers: Hans Flink, Chang Mei Lin
client: Alberto Culver
(*VO5*)

design firm: **Turner Duckworth**
San Francisco, California
designers: Bruce Duckworth, Bob Leliz
client: Neal's Yard

design firm: **Bailey Design Group, Inc.**
Plymouth Meeting, Pennsylvania
designers: Dave Fiedler, Tisha Armour
client: Johnson & Johnson
(*Johnson's Baby Oil Gel*)

design firm: **Bailey Design Group, Inc.**
Plymouth Meeting, Pennsylvania
designers: Dave Fiedler, Steve Perry
client: Johnson & Johnson
(*Clean & Clear*)

design firm: **Turner Duckworth**
San Francisco, California
designer: Bruce Duckworth
client: Superdrug

design firm: **Hans Flink Design**
New York, New York
designer: Chang Mei Lin
client: Chesebrough Ponds
(*Pears Aromatherapy*)

design firm: **Wickens Tutt Southgate**
London, England
designers: Wickens Tutt Southgate
client: Superdrug
(*Men's Aromatherapy*)

design firm: **Hans Flink Design Inc.**
New York, New York
designers: Hans D. Flink, Susan Clark,
Chang Mei Lin
client: Chesebrough-Pond's
(*Pond's Cosmetics*)

55

design firm: **Bailey Design Group, Inc.**
Plymouth Meeting, Pennsylvania
designers: Ken Cahill, Jeff Kowal
client: Jardine Foods
(7J Ranch)

design firm: **Ray Honda Design**
Petaluma, California
designer: Ray Honda
client: Cuisine Perel

design firm: **Mark Oliver, Inc.**
Santa Barbara, California
designers: Mark Oliver, Patty Devlin-Driskel
client: Appeteasers

design firm: **Babcock, Schmid,**
Louis & Partners
Bath, Ohio
client: Guggisberg Cheese

design firm: **Profile Design**
San Francisco, California
designers: Profile Design
client: JA Zenchu

design firm: **Ray Honda Design**
Petaluma, California
designer: Ray Honda
client: Cuisine Perel

design firm: **Michael•Nash Associates**
London, England
designers: Anthony Michael, Stephanie Nash
client: Harvey Nichols

design firm: **Turner Duckworth**
San Francisco, California
designer: Janice Davison
client: Waitrose

design firm: **Curtis Design**
San Francisco, California
designers: Dave Curtis, Chris Benitez
client: Fantastic Foods

design firm: **SBG Enterprise**
San Francisco, California
designer: Mary Brucken
client: Cole's

design firm: **Mark Oliver, Inc.**
Santa Barbara, California
designer: Mark Oliver
client: Crunchwells

design firm: **Mark Oliver, Inc.**
Santa Barbara, California
designer: Mark Oliver
client: San Luis Sourdough

design firm: **Elmwood**
             Leeds, England
designer: Carolyn Abson
client: CPC (UK) Ltd.

design firm: **Pearlfisher**
             London, England
creative director:
             Jonathan Ford
designers: Shaun Bowen, Sarah Butler
client: Whitworths

design firm: **Elmwood**
             Leeds, England
designers: Jon Stubley, Steve Shaw,
             Alison Beckwith
client: CPC (UK) Ltd.

design firm: **CRAYON Design & Communication**
Montreal, Canada
designers: Sol Lang, Mary Bogdan, Carl Prud'Homme
client: Msc International inc.

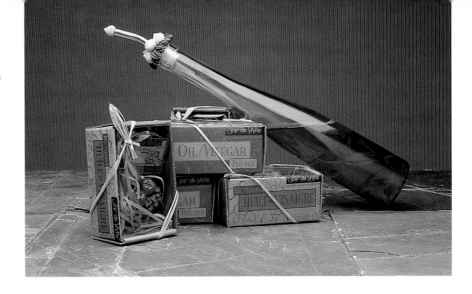

design firm: **Profile Design**
San Francisco, California
designers: Profile Design
client: Sun Garden Packing Company

design firm: **SBG Enterprise**
San Francisco, California
designer: Laura Cramer
client: Mann's

design firm: **Profile Design**
San Francisco, California
designers: Profile Design
client: Mrs. Field's

design firm: **Profile Design**
San Francisco, California
designers: Profile Design
client: Otis Spunkmeyer

design firm: **Chen Tsoi Design**
London, England
designers: Chen Tsoi, Kara Sims
client: Tesco

design firm: **Chen Tsoi Design**
London, England
designer: Kara Sims
client: Somerfield

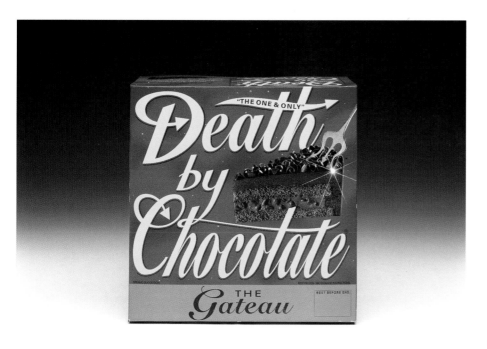

design firm: **Springetts**
London, England
designers: Springetts
client: Brossard
(*Death by Chocolate*)

design firm: **Dixon & Parcels Associates, Inc.**
            New York, New York
designers: Dixon & Parcels Associates
client: Campbell Soup Company

design firm: **Praxis Diseñadores Y Asoc., SC**
            Mexico, D.F.
designer: Alberto Flores
art director: Juan Carlos Rojas R.
client: Danone/Kellogg Co.

design firm: **Chen Tsoi Design**
            London, England
designer: Chen Tsoi
client: Somerfield

design firm: **Praxis Diseñadores Y Asociados, SC**
Mexico, D.F.
designer: Sandra Vazquez
art director: Juan Carlos Rojas R.
client: Kellogg De Mexico

design firm: **Profile Design**
San Francisco, California
designers: Profile Design
client: Safeway Stores, Inc.

design firm: **Profile Design**
San Francisco, California
designers: Profile Design
client: Kraft Foods

design firm: **Hornall Anderson Design Works, Inc.**
Seattle, Washington
designers: Jack Anderson, Jana Nishi
client: Seattle Chocolate Company

design firm: **SBG Enterprise**
San Francisco, California
designer: David Curtis
client: Quaker Oats

design firm: **Planet Design Co.**
Madison, Wisconsin
designers: Planet Design Co.
client: Candinas Chocolatier

66

design firm: **Thibault Paolini Design Assoc.**
Portland, Maine
designer: Judy Paolini
client: Zandhoeven

design firm: **Sayles Graphic Design**
Des Moines, Iowa
designer: John Sayles
client: Gianna Rose
(*Golden Egg*)

design firm: **Hornall Anderson Design Works, Inc.**
Seattle, Washington
designers: Jack Anderson, Jana Nishi,
Heidi Favour, David Bates,
Mary Hermes, Mary Chin Hutchison
client: Seattle Chocolate Company

design firm: **Hans Flink Design Inc.**
New York, New York
designers: Hans D. Flink, Jane Parasczak
client: Hofbauer Chocolates of Vienna

design firm: **Hornall Anderson Design Works, Inc.**
Seattle, Washington
designers: Jack Anderson, Jana Nishi, David Bates, Sonja Max
client: Cloud Nine

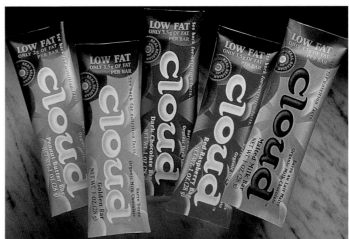

design firm: **Dixon & Parcels Associates, Inc.**
New York, New York
designers: Dixon & Parcels Associates, Inc.
client: Hershey Foods Corporation
(*"Hugs" Plain*)

design firm: **Hornall Anderson Design Works, Inc.**
Seattle, Washington
designers: Jack Anderson, Jana Nishi
client: Seattle Chocolate Company

design firm: **Hans Flink Design Inc.**
New York, New York
designers: Jaque Auger, Amy Atkinson
client: Nestlé
(*Candy Tops*)

design firm: **Dixon & Parcels Associates, Inc.**
New York, New York
designers: Dixon & Parcels Associates, Inc.
client: Hershey Foods Corporation
(*"Amazin' Fruit"*)

design firm: **Chen Tsoi Design**
London, England
designers: Chen Tsoi, Andrea Maloney
client: Tesco

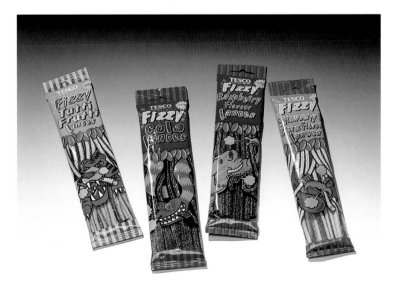

design firm: **Chen Tsoi Design**
London, England
designer: Chen Tsoi
client: Somerfield

design firm: **Mark Oliver, Inc.**
Santa Barbara, California
designers: Mark Oliver, Patty Devlin-Driskel
client: Desert Grove—Sweetnut

design firm: **Bailey Design Group, Inc.**
Plymouth Meeting, Pennsylvania
designers: Dave Fiedler, Steve Perry,
Gary La Croix
client: Jel Sert

70

design firm: **Mike Salisbury Communications**
Marina Del Rey, California
designer: Mike Salisbury

design firm: **Hornall Anderson Design Works, Inc.**
Seattle, Washington
designers: Jack Anderson, Debra McCloskey,
Margaret Long, Heidi Favour
client: Nordstrom

design firm: **Sibley Peteet Design**
Dallas, Texas
designer: Tom Kirsch
client: Frito Lay
(*Doritos*)

design firm: **Curtis Design**
San Francisco, California
designers: Dave Curtis, Fong Sung
client: Garden of Eatin'

design firm: **Colonna Farrell Design**
St. Helena, California
designers: Christina Baldwin, Yolanda Ng
client: Marie Callender's

design firm: **Klim Design Inc.**
Avon, Connecticut
designer: Matt Klim
client: Jalosco Food Co.

72

design firm: **Elmwood**
Leeds, England
designers: Martyn Hayes, Nick Hynes
client: Terry Suchard

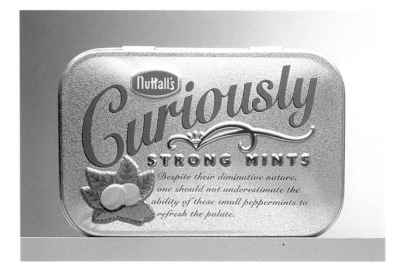

design firm: **Springetts**
London, England
designers: Springetts
client: Dairy Crest
(*Cathedral City Cheese*)

design firm: **Design Core Pty. Ltd.**
Adelaide, Australia
designer: Elizabeth Schlooz
production: Sergio Jeloscek
photography: Adam Bruzzone
client: Hog Bay Apiary
(*Kangaroo Island Honey*)

design firm: **Zebra Design**
                Fairport, New York
designers: James L. Selak, Tina Selak Klaus
client: Chase Manhattan Bank

design firm: **Tangram Strategic Design**
                Novara, Italy
creative director:
                Enrico Sempi
art director, designer:
                Antonella Trevisan
client: Briko S.r.l.
                (*Briko Sun-Glasse Sporteyes*)

design firm: **Tangram Strategic Design**
                Novara, Italy
creative director:
                Enrico Sempi
art director, designer:
                Antonella Trevisan
client: Briko S.r.l.
                (*Briko Ski and Bike Helmets*)

design firm: **Visual Asylum**
San Diego, California
designer: Amy Jo Levine
client: Troxel
(*ProAction*)

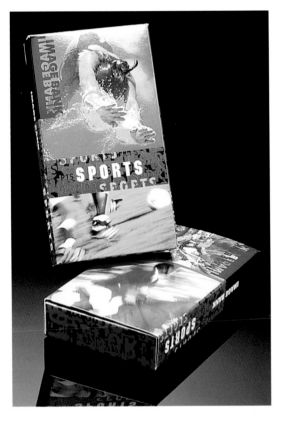

design firm: **Sibley Peteet Design**
Dallas, Texas
designer: Donna Aldridge
client: Image Bank

design firm: **Thibault Paolini Design Assoc.**
Portland, Maine
designer: Judy Paolini
client: Sportworks, Ltd.

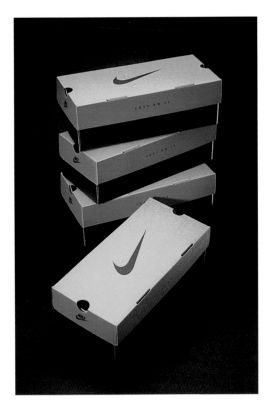

design firm: **Nike**
Beaverton, Oregon
designer: Jeff Weithman
client: Nike Corporate Packaging
(*Nike ACG Packaging*)

design firm: **Mires Design, Inc.**
San Diego, California
art director: José A. Serrano
designers: José A. Serrano, Miguel Perez
photographer: Carl Vanderschuit
client: Voit Sports

design firm: **Paragon Design International**
Chicago, Illinois
creative director:
Bob Gailen
project director:
John Racila
client: All American Products Co.

design firm: **Deskey Associates**
New York, New York
client: The Coleman Company

design firm: **Laura Coe Design Assoc.**
San Diego, California
designers: Laura Coe Wright, Denise Heisey
client: Taylor Made Golf

design firm: **Simon & Goetz**
Frankfurt, Germany
creative director:
Ruediger Goetz
designer: Elke Boehm
client: ADP engineering Gmbtt

design firm: **Paragon Design International**
Chicago, Illinois
creative director:
Bob Gailen
project director:
John Racila
client: All American Products Co.

design firm: **Laura Coe Design Associates**
San Diego, California
designers: Laura Coe Wright, Lauren Bruhn,
Ryoichi Yotsumoto
client: ProAction

design firm: **Mark Oliver, Inc.**
Santa Barbara, California
designer: Mark Oliver
client: Force Fin

(opposite)
design firm: **Mires Design, Inc.**
San Diego, California
art director: José A. Serrano
designers: José A. Serrano, Miguel Perez
photographer: Carl Vanderschuit
client: Voit Sports

design firm: **Tangram Strategic Design**
Novara, Italy
creative director:
Enrico Sempi
art directors: Antonella Trevisan, Enrico Sempi
designers: Antonella Trevisan, Anna Grimaldi
client: Briko S.r.l.

design firm: **Laura Coe Design Assoc.**
San Diego, California
designers: Lauren Bruhn, Ryoichi Yotsumoto
client: ProAction

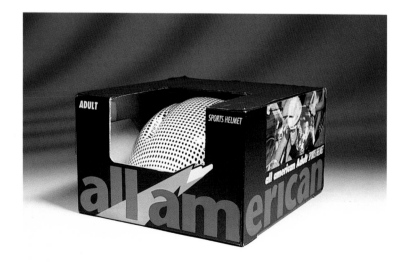

design firm: **Paragon Design International**
Chicago, Illinois
creative director:
Bob Gailen
project director:
John Racila
client: All American Products Co.

design firm: **Laura Coe Design Assoc.**
San Diego, California
designers: Lauren Bruhn, Darryl Glass
client: Titleist

design firm: **Laura Coe Design Assoc.**
San Diego, California
designers: Laura Coe Wright, Lauren Bruhn,
Carey Gerwig Jones
client: ProAction

design firm: **Segura Inc.**
Chicago, Illinois
designer: Carlos Segura
client: XXX Snowboards

design firm: **Simon & Goetz**
Frankfurt, Germany
creative director:
Ruediger Goetz
art director: Heike Brockmann
designer: Elke Boehm
client: SKF

design firm: **Riley Design Associates**
Danville, California
designers: Dan Riley, Pam Caudle, Vondra Doherty
client: Masterlock

design firm: **Tangram Strategic Design**
Novara, Italy
creative director:
Enrico Sempi
art director, designer:
Antonella Trevisan
client: Briko S.r.l.

82

design firm: **Planet Design Co.**
Madison, Wisconsin
designers: Planet Design Co.
client: Graber U.S.A.

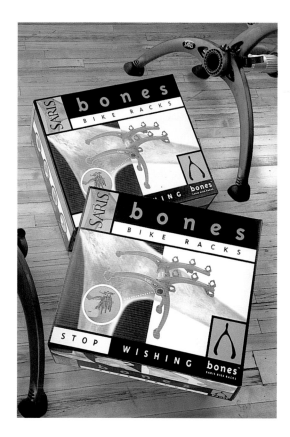

design firm: **Nicholson Design**
Encinitas, California
designer: Joe C. Nicholson
client: Fotoball

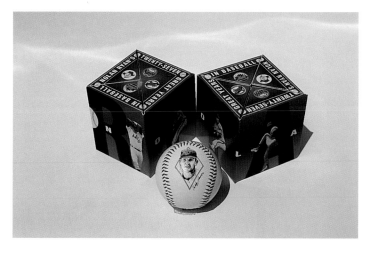

design firm: **Laura Coe Design Assoc.**
San Diego, California
designers: Laura Coe Wright, Ryoichi Yotsumoto
client: ProAction

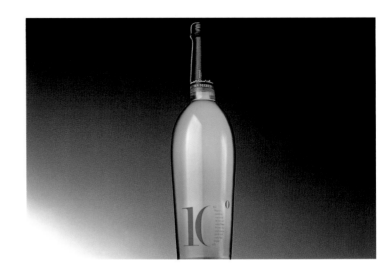

design firm: **Covey Porter Bell**
London, England
designer: Martin Grimer
client: Eden Valley Mineral Water

design firm: **Minale Tattersfield Designers**
Richmond, United Kingdom
designers: Minale Tattersfield Designers
client: Osotspa
(*Shark*)

design firm: **Hornall Anderson Design Works, Inc.**
Seattle, Washington
designers: Jack Anderson, Larry Anderson, Julie Keenan
client: Alta Beverage Company

design firm: **Blackburn's Ltd.**
London, England
designer: Kathy Miller
client: Waitrose

84

design firm: **Hans Flink Design Inc.**
New York, New York
designers: Denise Heisey, Chang Mei Lin
client: Mott's Cadbury Beverages

design firm: **Turner Duckworth**
San Francisco, California
designers: Bruce Duckworth, Janice Davison
client: Schweppes

design firm: **Blackburn's Ltd.**
London, England
designers: John Blackburn, Belinda Duggan, Roberta Oates
client: Gleneagles Spring Waters
(*Gleneagles Natural Mineral Water "Beneath the Rainbow"*)

design firm: **Turner Duckworth**
San Francisco, California
designers: Bruce Duckworth,
Janice Davison
client: British Steel

design firm: **Praxis Diseñadores Y Asoc., SC**
Mexico, D. F.
designer: Sandra Vazquez
art director: Nadya Villegas
client: Valle Redondo

design firm: **Dixon & Parcels Associates, Inc.**
New York, New York
designers: Dixon & Parcels Associates, Inc.
client: Citrus World, Inc.

design firm: **Praxis Diseñadores Y Asoc., SC**
Mexico, D.F.
designer: Sandra Vazquez
art director: Juan Carlos Rojas R.
client: Valle Redondo
(*Confruta Juices*)

design firm: **Chen Tsoi Design**
                London, England
designer: Chen Tsoi
client: Somerfield

design firm: **SBG Enterprise**
                San Francisco, California
designer: Jim Nevins
client: Welch's

design firm: **Chen Tsoi Design**
              London, England
designer: Chen Tsoi
client: Somerfield

design firm: **Tangram Strategic Design**
              Novara, Italy
creative director:
              Enrico Sempi
art director, designer:
              Antonella Trevisan
illustrator: Sergio Quaranta
client: Gruppo SUN
              (*Consilia*)

design firm: **Howe Design**
              Droylsden, England
graphic designer:
              James Smith
art director: Joe Howe
client: Barr Soft Drinks
              (*Sundaze Soft Drinks*)

design firm: **Howe Design**
Droylsden, England
designer: James Smith
art director: Joe Howe
client: Barr Soft Drinks
(*KA Soft Drinks*)

design firm: **Addison Design
Consultants Pte Ltd**
Singapore, Republic of Singapore
designer: Mohmad Noor Ariffin
client: Coca Cola Export Corporation

design firm: **Addison Design Consultants Pte Ltd**
Singapore, Republic of Singapore
designer: Keith Chan
client: F&N Coca-Cola Pte Ltd

design firm: **Hornall Anderson Design Works, Inc.**
Seattle, Washington
designers: Jack Anderson, Julia LaPine, Jill Bustamante
client: Talking Rain

design firm: **Pearlfisher**
London, England
designers: Jonathan Ford, Karen Welman
client: Pernod Ricard

design firm: **Hornall Anderson Design Works, Inc.**
Seattle, Washington
designers: Jack Anderson, Jana Nishi
client: Talking Rain

design firm: **Pearlfisher**
London, England
designers: Jonathan Ford, Lawrence Haggerty
client: Pearlfisher
(*Altitude Mineral Water*)

design firm: **Pearlfisher**
London, England
creative director:
Karen Welman
graphic designer:
Paula Patricola
client: Newby Teas

design firm: **Addison Design Consultants Pte Ltd.**
Singapore
designer: Julia Ng
client: Taikoo Sugar Ltd.
(*Premium Ceylon Tea*)

design firm: **Kan & Lau Design Consultants**
Hong Kong, Republic of China
creative director:
Kan Tai-keung
art directors: Kan Tai-keung, Eddy Yu Chi Kong
designer: Patrick Fung
client: Unilever Hong Kong Ltd

design firm: **Hans Flink Design Inc.**
New York, New York
designers: Steve Hooper, Mark Krukonis,
Chang Mei Lin
client: Kraft Foods, Inc.
(*MH Cappuccino*)

design firm: **Hornall Anderson Design Works, Inc.**
Seattle, Washington
designers: Jack Anderson, Julie Lock, Jana Nishi,
Julie Keenan, Lian Ng, Julia LaPine,
Mary Chin Hutchison
client: Starbucks Coffee Company

design firm: **Sayles Graphic Design**
Des Moines, Iowa
designer: John Sayles
client: Java Joes

design firm: **Springetts**
           London, England
designers: Springetts
client: MD Foods
           (*Gulp*)

design firm: **Michael•Nash Associates**
           London, England
designers: Anthony Michael, Stephanie Nash
client: Harvey Nichols

design firm: **Praxis Diseñadores Y Asoc., SC**
           Mexico, D.F.
designer: Hector Ariza
art director: Juan Carlos Rojas R.
client: Danone Mexico

design firm: **Puig Falco Associats**
Barcelona, Spain
art director: Sergi Puig
illustrator: Jordi Forcada
client: Condis

design firm: **Chen Tsoi Design**
London, England
designer: Chen Tsoi
client: Somerfield

design firm: **Springetts**
London, England
designers: Springetts
client: Dairy Crest
(*Frijj*)

95

design firm: **Bailey DesignGroup, Inc.**
                Plymouth Meeting, Pennsylvania
designers: Ken Cahill, Steve Perry,
                Jeff Behrenhauser
client: Maxell Corporation of America

design firm: **LMS Design**
                Stamford, Connecticut
designer: Richard Shear
client: Gemini Industries

design firm: **SBG Enterprise**
                San Francisco, California
designers: Philip Ting, Frank Szeto
client: Adaptec, Inc.

design firm: **Riley Design Associates**
            Danville, California
designers: Dan Riley, Vondra Doherty,
            German Lopez
client: Darwin Keyboards

design firm: **Mires Design, Inc.**
            San Diego, California
art director: José A. Serrano
designers: José A. Serrano, Deborah Hom
photographer: Carl Vanderschuit
client: Qualcomm

design firm: **Rickabaugh Graphics**
            Gahanna, Ohio
designer: Eric Rickabaugh
client: Nationwide Insurance

design firm: **SBG Enterprise**
                 San Francisco, California
designers: Mark Bergman, Margie Drechsel
client: The Learning Company

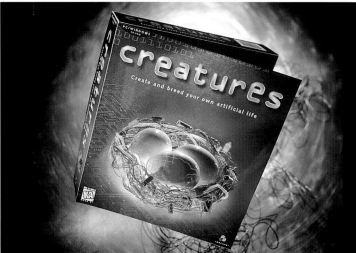

design firm: **Hal Apple Design**
                 Manhattan Beach, California
designers: Hal Apple Design

design firm: **Hornall Anderson Design Works, Inc.**
                 Seattle, Washington
designers: Jack Anderson, John Anicker, Margaret Long
client: Corbis Corporation

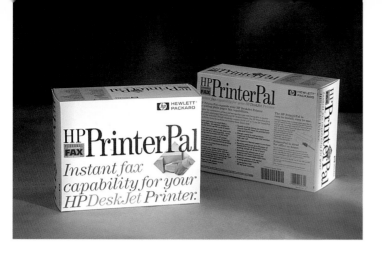

design firm: **Tharp Did It**
Los Gatos, California
designer: Rick Tharp
Tharp and Drummond Did It
client: Hewlett Packard

design firm: **Mires Design, Inc.**
San Diego, California
art director: John Ball
designers: John Ball, Miguel Perez
photographer: Marshall Harrington
client: Verde Communications

design firm: **Hornall Anderson Design Works, Inc.**
Seattle, Washington
designers: Jack Anderson, John Anicker, David Bates
client: Corbis Corporation

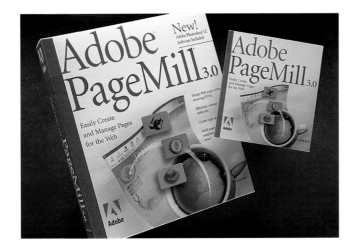

design firm: **Hornall Anderson Design Works, Inc.**
Seattle, Washington
designers: Jack Anderson, Katha Dalton,
Jana Wilson Esser, Jana Nishi, Julie Lock
client: Adobe Corporation

design firm: **Sibley Peteet Design**
Dallas, Texas
designer: Tom Hough
client: Nortel

design firm: **Mires Design, Inc.**
San Diego, California
art director: Scott Mires
designer, illustrator:
Miguel Perez
photographer: Mike Campos
client: Jabra Corporation

design firm: **Mires Design, Inc.**
San Diego, California
art director: John Ball
designers: John Ball, Eric Freedman
illustrators: Bill Morrison, Eric Freedman
client: Comptons New Media

design firm: **Hal Apple Design**
Manhattan Beach, California
designers: Hal Apple Design

design firm: **Thibault Paolini Design Assoc.**
Portland, Maine
designer: Judy Paolini
client: Woodkrafter Kits

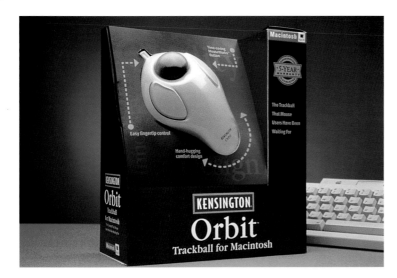

design firm: **SBG Enterprise**
             San Francisco, California
designer: Paul Chock
client: Kensington Microware Limited

design firm: **Mike Salisbury Communications**
             Marina Del Rey, California
designer: Mike Salisbury

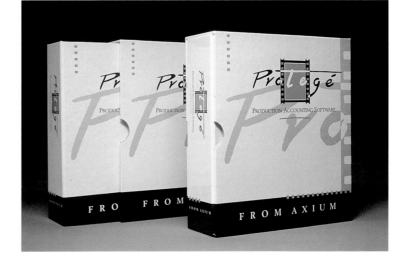

design firm: **H2D**
             Milwaukee, Wisconsin
designer: Allan Haas
client: Motorola

design firm: **Hornall Anderson Design Works, Inc.**
Seattle, Washington
designers: John Hornall, Mary Hermes, Jana Nishi,
Virginia Le, Mary Chin Hutchison
client: Allaire Corporation

design firm: **Critique**
Palo Alto, California
designers: Marty Neumeier, Chris Chu
client: Legal Point

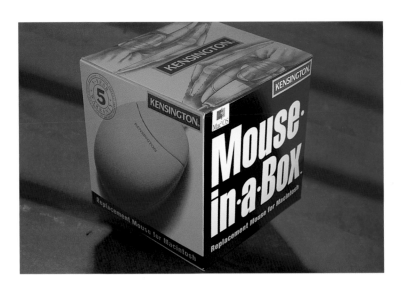

design firm: **SBG Enterprise**
San Francisco, California
designer: Thomas Bond
client: Kensington Technology Group

design firm: **Bailey Design Group, Inc.**
Plymouth Meeting, Pennsylvania
designers: Ken Cahill, Steve Perry
client: Omnipoint Communications
(*Omnipoint QuicKit*)

design firm: **Hal Apple Design**
Manhattan Beach, California
designers: Hal Apple Design

design firm: **Hornall Anderson Design Works, Inc.**
Seattle, Washington
designers: Jack Anderson, Mary Hermes,
Mary Chin Hutchison, Margaret Long,
Debra McCloskey
client: AirTouch Cellular

design firm: **Platinum Design, Inc.**
               New York, New York
designer: Kathleen Phelps
client: Time Warner Electronic Publishing

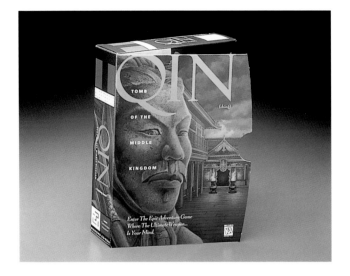

design firm: **SBG Enterprise**
               San Francisco, California
designer: Philip Ting
client: Global Communications, Inc.

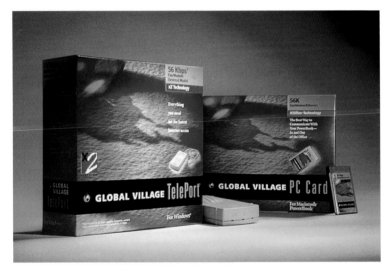

design firm: **A Free Hand**
               Lexington, Kentucky
designers: Paula Gron/Clark Typesetting
client: Multi-Link, Inc.
               Michael Murray, Marketing

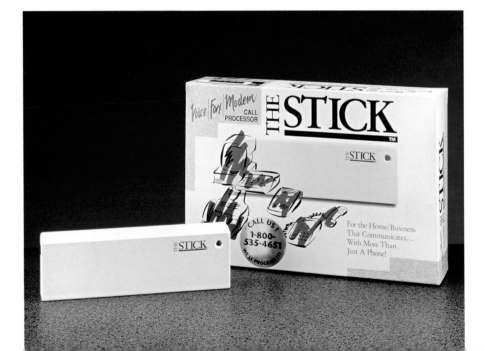

design firm: **Hornall Anderson Design Works, Inc.**
             Seattle, Washington
designers: Jack Anderson, Debra McCloskey, Heidi Favour,
             Jana Wilson Esser, Larry Anderson, Nicole Bloss
client: Novell, Inc.

design firm: **Hornall Anderson Design Works, Inc.**
             Seattle, Washington
designers: Jack Anderson, Jana Nishi,
             Heidi Favour, David Bates, Sonja Max
client: Resource Games

design firm: **Triad, Inc.**
             Larkspur, California
designers: Michael Dambrowski, Michael Hinshaw
client: Silton-Bookman Systems Inc.

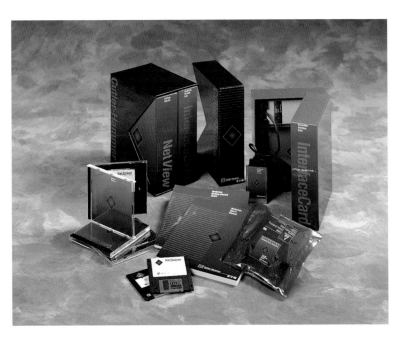

design firm: **H2D**
Milwaukee, Wisconsin
designers: Allan Haas, Joe Hausch
client: Cutler Hammer/Eaton Corporation

design firm: **Profile Design**
San Francisco, California
designers: Profile Design
client: Ascend Communications

design firm: **Sayles Graphic Design**
Des Moines, Iowa
designer: John Sayles
client: ImMix Video Cube

107

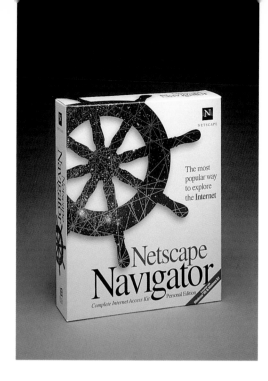

design firm: **Critique**
Palo Alto, California
designers: Marty Neumeier, Chris Chu, Heather McDonald
client: Netscape

design firm: **Critique**
Palo Alto, California
designers: Marty Neumeier, Chris Chu,
David Wilcox
client: Claris

design firm: **Critique**
Palo Alto, California
designers: Marty Neumeier, Chris Chu,
Vinh Chung
client: Zydeco

design firm: **Critique**
Palo Alto, California
designers: Marty Neumeier, Chris Chu,
Heather McDonald
client: Pointcast

design firm: **Babcock, Schmid, Louis & Partners**
Bath, Ohio
client: Alpha

design firm: **Visual Asylum**
San Diego, California
designers: MaeLin Levine, Amy Jo Levine
client: The Lightspan Partnership

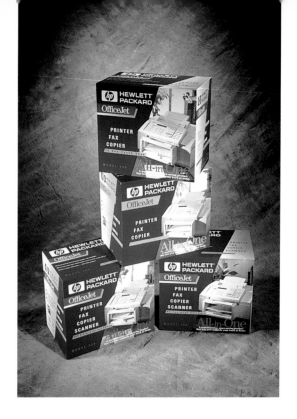

design firm: **Babcock, Schmid, Louis & Partners**
Bath, Ohio
client: Alpha

design firm: **Wilson-Lewis-Wilson Design**
Palm Harbor, Florida
designer: Bill Wilson
client: Allied Digital Technologies

design firm: **Oden Marketing & Design**
Memphis, Tennessee
design director:
Michael Guthrie
designer: Liz Allen
creative director:
Bret Terwilleger
client: International Paper

design firm: **Oden Marketing & Design**
Memphis, Tennessee
design director:
Michael Guthrie
designers: Michael Guthrie, Bill Berry, Liz Allen,
Billy Riley, Ashley Toporek
creative director:
Bret Terwilleger
writer: Brenda Trigg
client: International Paper

design firm: **Hornall Anderson Design Works, Inc.**
Seattle, Washington
designers: John Hornall, Larry Anderson, Jana Nishi
client: Attachmate Corporation

design firm: **Watt, Roop & Co.**
Cleveland, Ohio
designer: Kurt R. Roscoe
client: Steel Service Center Institute

111

design firm: **Bailey Design Group, Inc.**
Plymouth Meeting, Pennsylvania
designers: Ken Cahill, Steve Perry, Gary La Croix
client: Maxell Corporation of America
(*Maxell Video*)

design firm: **Critique**
Palo Alto, California
designers: Marty Neumeier, Chris Chu,
Eric Todd, Vinh Chung
client: Autodesk

design firm: **Riley Design Associates**
Danville, California
designers: Dan Riley, Vondra Doherty
client: PinPoint Software, Inc.

design firm: **Riley Design Associates**
Danville, California
art director: Dan Riley
designers: Vondra Doherty, German Lopez
client: Kensington

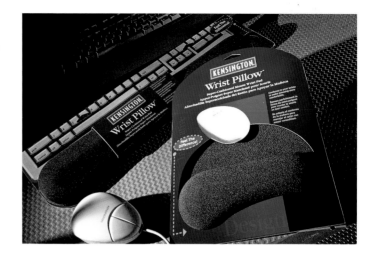

design firm: **Laura Coe Design Assoc.**
San Diego, California
designer: Lauren Bruhn
client: Laura Coe Design Assoc.

design firm: **Perceive, LLC**
Long Beach, California
designers: Nora Singer,
Jamie Graupner
client: IVS

113

design firm: **Joss**
Chicago, Illinois
designer: Adrienne Muryn
client: Nortel

design firm: **SBG Enterprise**
San Francisco, California
designer: chris golmer
client: Autodesk

design firm: **Giles Design, Inc.**
San Antonio, Texas
designers: Jill Giles, Barbara Schelling,
Warren Borror
client: Metrowerks

114

design firm: **After Hours Creative**
Phoenix, Arizona
designers: After Hours Creative
client: After Hours Creative

design firm: **FUSE, Inc.**
Atlanta, Georgia
designers: Rich Godfrey, Pete Rundquist,
Joanna Duryea
client: IBM

design firm: **A Free Hand**
Lexington, Kentucky
designers: Paula Gron, Jerri Self
client: Multi-Link, Inc.

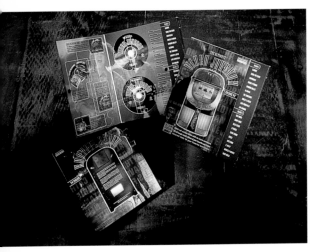

design firm: **After Hours Creative**
Phoenix, Arizona
designers: After Hours Creative
client: After Hours Creative

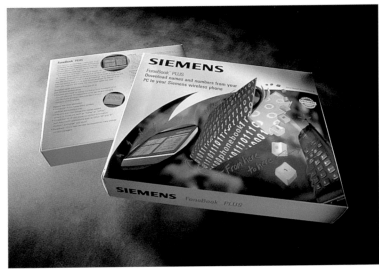

design firm: **Sibley Peteet Design**
Dallas, Texas
designer: Art Garcia
client: Siemens Wireless Terminals

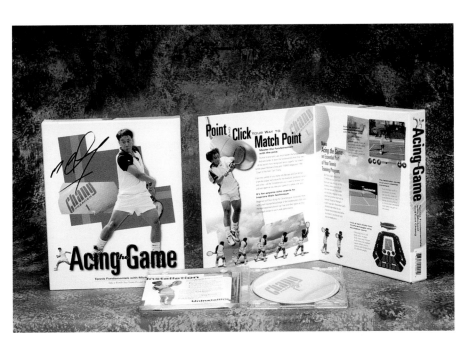

design firm: **Marketing by Design**
Sacramento, California
designers: Candy Thompson, Joel Stinghen
client: Center Court Productions

design firm: **DSI/LA**
Baton Rouge, Louisiana
designer: Nicole Duet
client: Xenetech, Inc.

design firm: **Sibley Peteet Design**
Dallas, Texas
designer: Donna Aldridge
client: Image Bank

design firm: **Kollberg/Johnson**
New York, New York
designers: Kollberg/Johnson
client: The Topps Co.

design firm: **Mike Salisbury Communications**
Marina Del Rey, California
designer: Mike Salisbury

design firm: **Mike Salisbury Communications**
Marina Del Rey, California
designer: Mike Salisbury

design firm: **Yokotake Design**
Venice, California
designer: Mike Yokotake
client: Exclusive Toy Products

design firm: **Sibley Peteet Design**
Dallas, Texas
designer: Don Sibley
client: Milton Bradley
(*Taboo*)

design firm: **Sibley Peteet Design**
Dallas, Texas
designer: John Evans
client: Milton Bradley
(*Scattergories*)

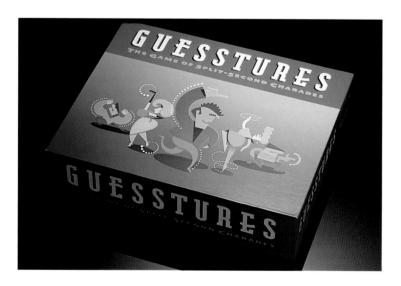

design firm: **Sibley Peteet Design**
Dallas, Texas
designer: David Beck
client: Milton Bradley
(*Guesstures*)

design firm: **Mires Design, Inc.**
San Diego, California
art director, designer:
José A. Serrano
illlutrator: Mark Frederickson
client: Upper Deck

design firm: **Hal Apple Design**
Manhattan Beach, California
designers: Hal Apple Design

design firm: **Thibault Paolini Design Assoc.**
Portland, Maine
designer: Sue Schenning Ryan
client: Little Harbor

design firm: **Hornall Anderson Design Works, Inc.**
    Seattle, Washington
designers: Jana Nishi, Sonja Max
client: Resource Games

design firm: **Mires Design, Inc.**
    San Diego, California
art director, designer:
    Scott Mires
illustrator: Tracy Sabin
client: Harcourt Brace & Co.

design firm: **Sayles Graphic Design**
    Des Moines, Iowa
designer: John Sayles
client: Pentech "Leadheads"

design firm: **Mires Design, Inc.**
San Diego, California
art director: Scott Mires
designer: Kathy Carpentier-Moore
illustrator: Tracy Sabin
client: Weber Costello

design firm: **Hal Apple Design**
Manhattan Beach, California
designers: Hal Apple Design

design firm: **Michael Osborne Design**
San Francisco, California
art director: Michael Osborne
designers: Michael Osborne Design
client: Sanford Corp.

123

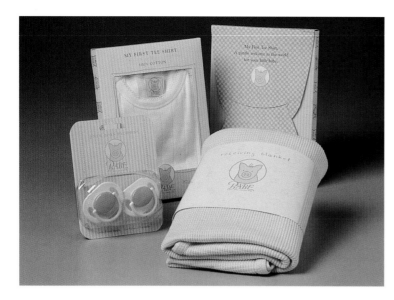

design firm: **Giles Design, Inc.**
San Antonio, Texas
designers: Jill Giles, Stephen Arevalos,
Barbara Schelling
client: Universal Studios

design firm: **Cato Design Inc.**
RIchmond, Australia
designers: Cato Design Inc.
client: Tupperware

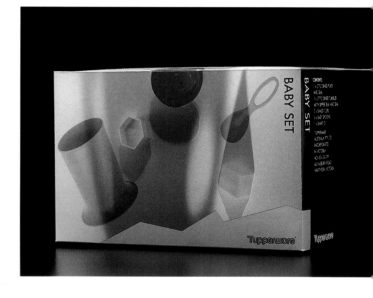

design firm: **Addison Design Consultants Pte Ltd**
Singapore, Republic of Singapore
client: International Nutrition Company

(*opposite*)
design firm: **Elmwood**
Guiseley Leeds, England
designers: Ben Greengrass,
Jonathan Lynch,
Jon Stubley
client: Asda Stores Ltd.

ASDA
baby

MUM APPROVED
HELPS BABY BREATHE CLEARLY

clearbreathe
bath

300ml

design firm: **Hornall Anderson Design Works, Inc.**
Seattle, Washington
designers: Jack Anderson, David Bates
client: Smith Sport Optics, Inc.

design firm: **Riley Design Associates**
Danville, California
designer: Dan Riley
client: Blacksmith Works

design firm: **Hal Apple Design**
Manhattan Beach, California
designers: Hal Apple Design
client: Ad One

design firm: **Hornall Anderson
Design Works, Inc.**
Seattle, Washington
designers: John Hornall, Julia LaPine, Heidi Favour,
Bruce Branson-Meyer, Jill Bustamante
client: Callanen International

design firm: **Hal Apple Design**
Manhattan Beach, California
designers: Hal Apple Design

design firm: **Hal Apple Design**
Manhattan Beach, California
designers: Hal Apple Design
client: Skechers

design firm: **Minale Tattersfield Designers**
Richmond, England
designers: Minale Tattersfield Designers
client: Bally

design firm: **Hal Apple Design**
Manahattan Beach, California
designers: Hal Apple Design

design firm: **Chen Tsoi Design**
              London, England
designer: Chen Tsoi
client: Tesco

design firm: **Turner Duckworth**
              San Francisco, California
designers: Jeff Fassnacht, David Turner
client: Levi Strauss & Co.

design firm: **Hal Apple Design**
              Manhattan Beach, California
designers: Hal Apple Design

129

design firm: **Wickens Tutt Southgate**
London, England
designers: Wickens Tutt Southgate
client: Gossard
(*Ultrabras*)

design firm: **Tangram Strategic Design**
Novara, Italy
creative director, art director:
Enrico Sempi
designers: Enrico Sempi, Anna Grimaldi
photographer: Edoardo Mari
client: Briko S.r.l.

design firm: **Turner Duckworth**
San Francisco, California
designers: David Turner, Brian Cox
client: Levi Strauss & Co.

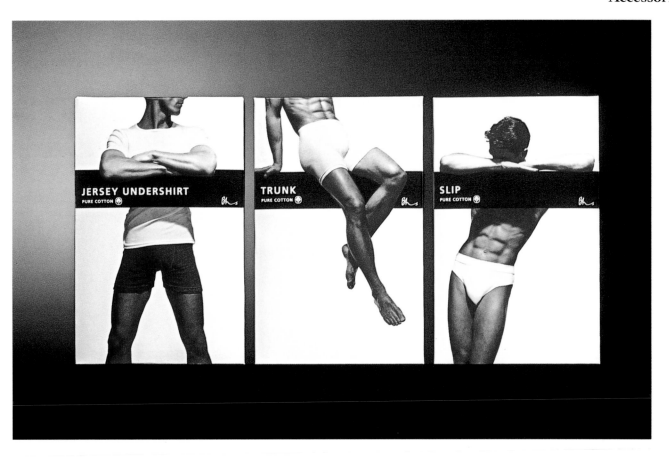

design firm: **Wickens Tutt Southgate**
         London, England
designers: Wickens Tutt Southgate
client: British Home Stores (Bhs)
         (*Mens Essentials*)

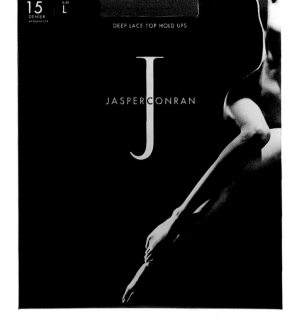

design firm: **David Richmond Associates**
         London, England
designers: Dave Richmond, David Gray, Andrew Tiller
client: Desenhams/Jasper Conran

design firm: **LMS Design**
Stamford, Connecticut
designer: Richard Shear
client: Brookstone

design firm: **David Richmond Associates**
London, England
designers: Dave Richmond, David Grah
client: Debenhams

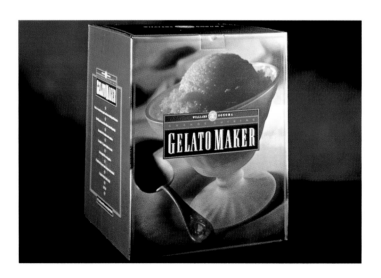

design firm: **SBG Enterprise**
San Francisco, California
designer: Paul Chock
client: Williams-Sonoma

design firm: **Michael Osborne Design**
San Francisco, California
designers: Michael Osborne Design
client: Nordstrom

design firm: **SBG Enterprise**
San Francisco, California
designer: Paul Chock
client: Williams–Sonoma

design firm: **Chen Tsoi Design**
London, England
designer: Andrea Maloney
client: Tesco

133

design firm: **Hornall Anderson Design Works, Inc.**
                Seattle, Washington
designers: Jack Anderson, Heidi Favour,
                John Anicker, David Bates
client: OXO, Int'l.

design firm: **Michael Orr + Associates, Inc.**
                Corning, New York
designers: Thomas Freeland, Michael R. Orr
client: Robinson Knife Company

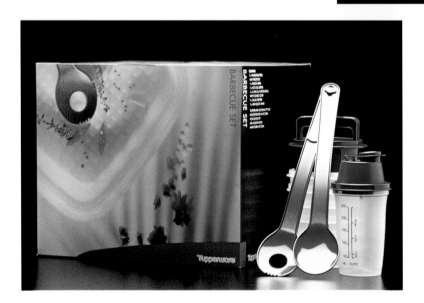

design firm: **Cato Design Inc.**
                Richmond, Australia
designers: Cato Design, Inc.
client: Tupperware

134

design firm: **Riley Design Associates**
               Danville, California
designers: Dan Riley, Vondra Doherty
photographer: Collopy-Vano
client: Kaiser

design firm: **Pearlfisher**
               London, England
designers: Karen Welman, Nina Hansen
client: Pearlfisher

design firm: **Riley Design Associates**
               Danville, California
art director, designer:
               Dan Riley
photographer: Collopy-Vano
client: Berndes-Kaiser

design firm: **R. Bird & Company**
New York, New York
designers: Joe Favata, Kevin Lenahan
client: Lever Brothers Company

design firm: **Hans Flink Design Inc.**
New York, New York
designers: Mark Krukonis, Susan Kunschaft
client: Colgate Palmolive
(*Fab*)

design firm: **R. Bird & Company**
New York, New York
designers: Joe Favata, Michele Li, Kevin Lenahan
client: Lever Brothers Company

design firm: **Springetts**
London, England
designers: Springetts
client: Jeyes
(*Parozone*)

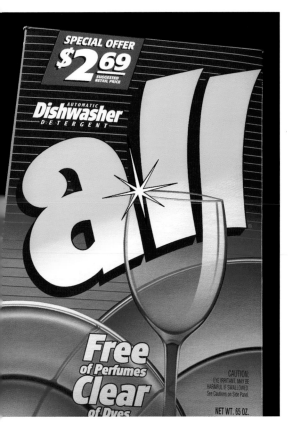

design firm: **Hans Flink Design Inc.**
New York, New York
designers: Chang Mei Lin, Jaque Auger
client: Unilever HPC
(*all*)

design firm: **Hans Flink Design Inc.**
New York, New York
designers: Gina Spears, Chang Mei Lin
client: Unilever HPC
(*Final Touch*)

design firm: **Cato Design Inc.**
Richmond, Australia
designers: Cato Design Inc.
client: Ampol

design firm: **Kilmer & Kilmer, Inc.**
Albuquerque, New Mexico
designers: Richard Kilmer, Gary Kohlman
client: Avonite

design firm: **Bailey Design Group, Inc.**
Plymouth Meeting, Pennsylvania
designers: Ken Cahill, Jeff Kowal
client: Walmart
(*Tech 2000*)

design firm: **Mires Design, Inc.**
San Diego, California
art director, designer:
Scott Mires
illustrator: Tracy Sabin
client: LA Gear

design firm: **Cato Design Inc.**
Richmond, Australia
designers: Cato Design Inc.
client: Ampol

139

design firm: **Gordon Randall Perry Design, Inc.**
New York, New York
bottle designer:
Gordon Randall Perry
graphic designer:
Bic's Staff
client: Bic Corp.

design firm: **Thibault Paolini Design Assoc.**
Portland, Maine
designer: Judy Paolini
client: Biddeford Mills

design firm: **Mires Design, Inc.**
San Diego, California
art director, designer:
José A. Serrano
illustrator: Tracy Sabin
client: Cranford Street

design firm: **Landor Associates**
London, England
designers: Landor Associates
client: Philips Lighting

design firm: **Riley Design Associates**
Danville, California
designers: Dan Riley, Vondra Doherty, Steve Ku
client: Day-Timer Technologies

design firm: **CDP Japan Ltd. Advertising**
Tokyo, Japan
creative director:
Takaaki Otani
designer: Masuhiro Maruyama
photographer: Masaru Mera
client: Matsushita Electric Works, Ltd.

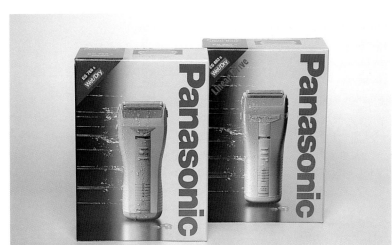

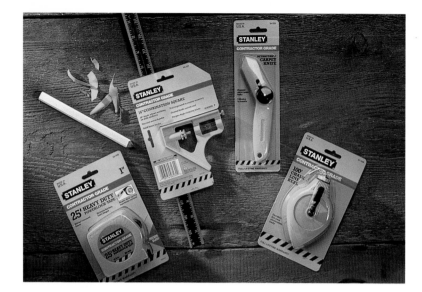

design firm: **Deskey Associates**
New York, New York
client: Stanley Tools

design firm: **Sibley Peteet Design**
Dallas, Texas
designer: Joy Cathey Price
client: Genie—Overhead Door

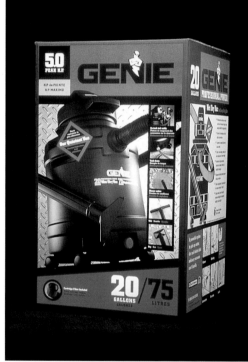

design firm: **Hornall Anderson Design Works, Inc.**
Seattle, Washington
designers: Jack Anderson, Lisa Cerveny, Bruce Branson-Meyer, Alan Florsheim
client: Custom Building Products

design firm: **Mires Design, Inc.**
San Diego, California
art director, designer:
José A. Serrano
illustrators: Tracy Sabin, Nancy Stahl
client: Deleo Clay Tile Company

design firm: **Mires Design, Inc.**
San Diego, California
art director: José A. Serrano
designer: Miguel Perez
illustrator: Tracy Sabin
client: Deleo Clay Tile Company

design firm: **Joss**
Chicago, Illinois
designers: Adrienne Muryn,
Rahn Farnum,
Dan Schuler
illustrator: Chris Deutchmann
client: Elmer's Products

design firm: **Group four Design**
               Avon, Connecticut
client: Prestone

design firm: **Deskey Associates**
               New York, New York
client: Angelo Brothers Company

design firm: **Cato Design Inc.**
               Richmond, Australia
designers: Cato Design Inc.
client: Nationalpak

design firm: **Group four Design**
Avon, Connecticut
client: Alsons Corporation

design firm: **Tom Fowler, Inc.**
Stamford, Connecticut
designer: Elizabeth P. Ball
client: Chesebrough-Pond's USA Co.

design firm: **Praxis Diseñadores Y Asociados, SC**
Mexico, D.F.
designer: Nadya Villegas
art director: Juan Carlos Rojas R.
client: Promeco Laboratory

design firm: **David Richmond Associates**
London, England
designers: Dave Richmond, David Gray
client: Elida Faberlié

design firm: **David Morris Creative Inc.**
Jersey City, New Jersey
designer: Chris Fuller
client: Caswell–Massey

design firm: **R. Bird & Company**
New York, New York
designers: Michele Li, Joe Favata
client: Lever Brothers Company

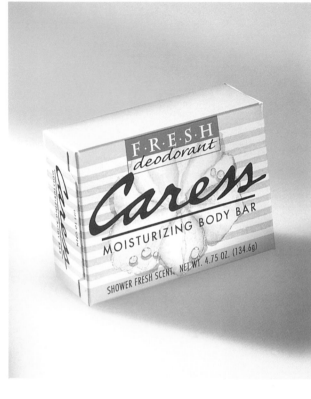

design firm: **R. Bird & Company**
New York, New York
designers: Michele Li, Joe Favata
client: Lever Brothers Company

design firm: **R. Bird & Company**
New York, New York
designers: Michele Li, Joe Favata
client: Lever Brothers Company

design firm: **Hans Flink Design Inc.**
New York, New York
designer: Hans D. Flink, Chang Mei Lin,
Mark Krukonis
client: Bayer Corp.
(*Stridex*)

design firm: **Bailey Design Group, Inc.**
Plymouth Meeting, Pennsylvania
designers: Dave Fiedler, Lauren Dunoff,
Christian Williamson
client: Johnson & Johnson
(*Shower to Shower*)

design firm: **Hans Flink Design Inc.**
New York, New York
designers: Susan Kunschaft, Mike Troian,
Mark Krukonis, Chang Mei Lin
client: Unilever HPC
(*Lever 2000*)

design firm: **Riley Design Associates**
Danville, California
designers: Dan Riley, Vondra Doherty
client: Lobob Labs, Inc.

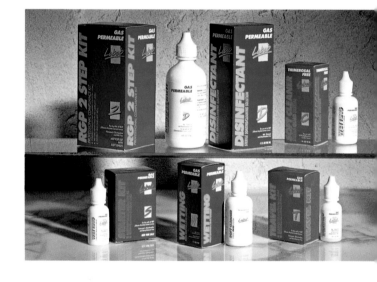

design firm: **Hans Flink Design Inc.**
New York, New York
designers: Susan Kunschaft, Mike Troian
client: Alberto Culver
(*FDS Stay Fresh*)

(*opposite*)
design firm: **Hans Flink Design Inc.**
New York, New York
designers: Hans D. Flink, Chang Mei Lin
client: Unilever HPC
(*Mentadent*)

design firm: **Tiangsu International Advertising Corp.**
Nanjing, Peoples Republic of China
art director: Dujun
client: Tiangsu Silk Imp. & Exp. Group Co., Ltd.

design firm: **Mike Salisbury Communications**
Marina Del Rey, California
designer: Mike Salisbury

design firm: **Mike Salisbury Communications**
Marina Del Rey, California
designer: Mike Salisbury

design firm: **Sayles Graphic Design**
Des Moines, Iowa
designers: John Sayles
client: Alphabet Soup

design firm: **David Richmond Associates**
London, England
designers: Dave Richmond, Dave Gram
client: Debenhams/Jasper Conran

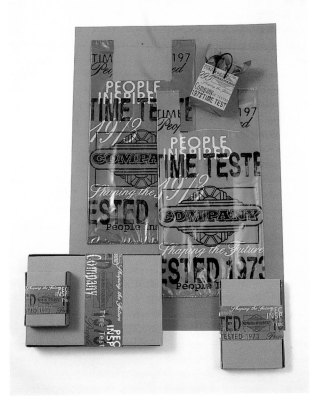

design firm: **Graphic Design**
Rio De Janeiro, Brazil
designer: Maria Wiza Goncalves Veiga Brito
client: Company Fashion Store

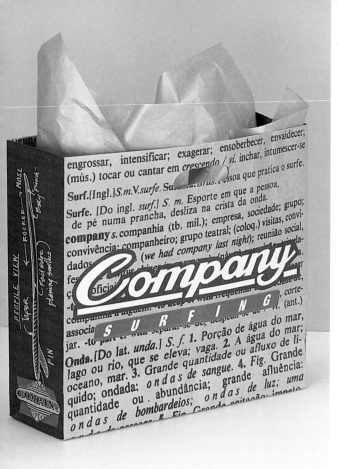

design firm: **Graphic Design**
               Rio De Janeiro, Brazil
designer: Maria Luiza Gonçalves Veiga Brito
client: Company Fashion Store

design firm: **Sayles Graphic Design**
               Des Moines, Iowa
designer: John Sayles
client: Schaffers Bridal Shop

design firm: **Donovan and Green**
               New York, New York
designer: Nancye Green
client: Barneys New York

design firm: **CDT Design**
London, England
art director: Neil Walker
Mac designer: Mike Dyer
client: Virgin

design firm: **CDT Design**
London, England
art director: Neil Walker
Mac designer: Mike Dyer
client: Virgin

design firm: **Dixon & Parcels Associates, Inc.**
New York, New York
designers: (patented by) J. Roy Parcels, Laurence Brulin
client: Holland Rantos Co.,
division of Youngs Drug Products
(*World's first self-hinged plastic {polypropylene} package—many cosmetic compacts, tube caps, bottle and jar lids plus rectangular-shaped cartons are using this technology.*)

design firm: **CDT Design**
London, England
art director: Neil Walker
Mac designer: Mike Dyer
client: Virgin

design firm: **Laura Coe Design Assoc.**
San Diego, California
designers: Laura Coe Wright,
Ryoichi Yotsumoto, Darryl Glass
client: Hewlett-Packard

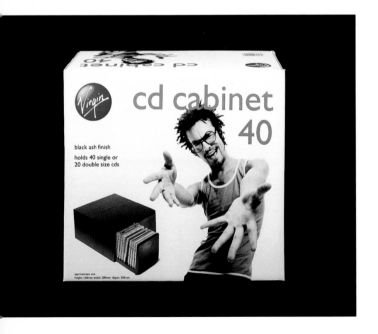

design firm: **Babcock, Schmid, Louis & Partners**
              Bath, Ohio
client: Alpha

design firm: **Giles Design, Inc.**
              San Antonio, Texas
designers: Jill Giles, Stephen Arevalos
client: Kathleen Sommers

design firm: **Dixon & Parcels Associates, Inc.**
              New York, New York
designers: J. Roy Parcels, George Woolley,
              (patented by) J. Roy Parcels, George Woolley
client: Trenton Folding Box Co.
              (*The world's first "pillow pack" folding carton,
              this patented package is produced on regular
              folding carton equipment. The basic
              construction is used in many different sizes
              and can be found in North America, Europe,
              and Asia for food, apparel, and promotions.
              Many hotels offer toiletries to their guests in
              this style of carton.*)

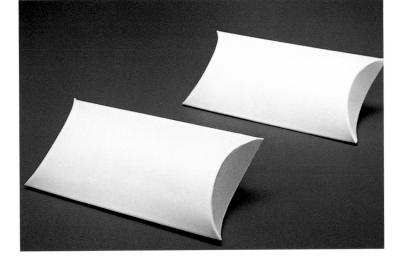

design firm: **HEBE. Werbung & Design**
Leonberg, Germany
creative director, writer:
Reiner Hebe
art director, designer:
Simone Rees
photographer: Werner Pawlok
client: E. Breuninger GmbH & Co.

design firm: **HEBE. Werbung & Design**
Leonberg, Germany
art directors: Reiner Hebe, Simone Rees
creative director, writer:
Reiner Hebe
designer: Simone Rees
client: Schuhhaus Werdich GmbH & Co.

158

design firm: **Hal Apple Design**
Manhattan Beach, California
designers: Hal Apple Design

design firm: **Tharp Did It**
Los Gatos, California
designer: Rick Tharp
client: The Gap (prototype)

design firm: **Gunnar Swanson Design Office**
Davis, California
designer: Gunnar Swanson
client: Standard Homeopathic Company
(*Specialty Medicines*)

design firm: **Thibault Paolini Design Assoc.**
Portland, Maine
designer: Judy Paolini
illustrator: Douglas Schneider
client: Global Health Alternatives
(*Vitalpath*)

design firm: **Hans Flink Design Inc.**
New York, New York
designers: Mark Krukonis, Hans D. Flink
client: Bayer Corp.
(*Neo-Synephrine*)

design firm: **Hal Apple Design**
Manhattan Beach, California
designers: Hal Apple Design

design firm: **Hal Apple Design**
Manhattan Beach, California
designers: Hal Apple Design

design firm: **Turner Duckworth**
San Francisco, California
designers: Bruce Duckworth
client: Superdrug

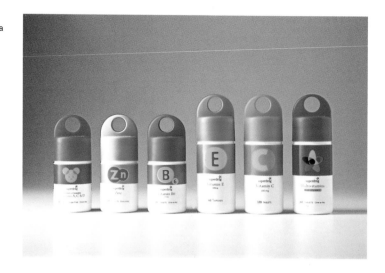

(opposite)
design firm: **After Hours Creative**
Phoenix, Arizona
designers: After Hours Creative
client: After Hours Creative

design firm: **Winson & Terry Design Consultants**
Republic of Singapore
designers: Sam Hong, Perry Tan
client: Winson & Terry

design firm: **Rickabaugh Graphics**
Gahanna, Ohio
designer: Mark Krumel
client: Cordage Papers

design firm: **Wilson-Lewis-Wilson Design**
Palm Harbor, Florida
designers: Bill Wilson, Beth Lewis-Wilson
client: Wilson-Lewis-Wilson

design firm: **Hal Apple Design**
Manhattan Beach, California
designers: Hal Apple Design

design firm: **Michael Osborne Design**
San Francisco, California
art director: Michael Osborne
designers: Michael Osborne Design
client: Michael Osborne Design

design firm: **Kilmer & Kilmer, Inc.**
Albuquerque, New Mexico
designers: Richard Kilmer, Randall Marshall,
Gary Kohlman
client: Kilmer & Kilmer
(*Holiday Promotion*)

design firm: **Mires Design, Inc.**
San Francisco, California
art director: José A. Serrano
designers: José A. Serrano, Miguel Perez
illustrator: Dan Thoner
client: Green Field Paper Company

design firm: **Greteman Group**
Wichita, Kansas
creative director:
Sonia Greteman
art directors: Sonia Greteman, James Strange
designers: James Strange, Jo Quillin
finishing artist: Jo Quillin
client: Costa Rica Natural Paper/coffee

design firm: **Greteman Group**
Wichita, Kansas
creative director:
Sonia Greteman
art directors: Sonia Greteman, James Strange
designers: James Strange, Jo Quillin
finishing artist: Jo Quillin
client: Costa Rica Natural Paper/banana

design firm: **Greteman Group**
        Wichita, Kansas
creative director:
        Sonia Greteman
art directors: Sonia Greteman, James Strange
designers: James Strange, Jo Quillin
finishing artist: Jo Quillin
client: Costa Rica Natural Paper/cigar

design firm: **Greteman Group**
        Wichita, Kansas
creative director:
        Sonia Greteman
art directors: Sonia Greteman, James Strange
designer: James Strange
finishing artist: Jo Quillin
client: Costa Rica Natural Paper—cigar box stationery

design firm: **Hal Apple Design**
        Manhattan Beach, California
designers: Hal Apple Design
client: Mead

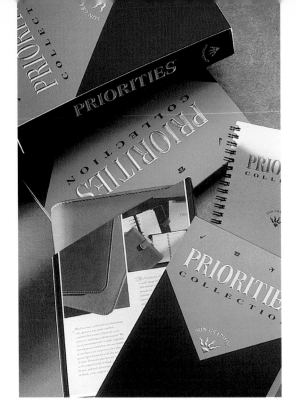

design firm: **Thibault Paolini Design Assoc.**
Portland, Maine
designer: Sue Schenning Ryan
client: Sun Graphix

design firm: **Visual Asylum**
San Diego, California
designers: Amy Jo Levine, MaeLin Levine
client: Digigami

design firm: **Michael • Nash Associates**
London, England
designers: Stephanie Nash, Anthony Michael
client: egg

(opposite)
design firm: **Kilmer & Kilmer, Inc.**
Albuquerque, New Mexico
designers: Richard Kilmer, Randall Marshall,
Gary Kohlman, Clint Batte,
Brenda Kilmer
writer: Don McKinney
client: Kilmer & Kilmer Journal

design firm: **Tom Dolle Design**
New York, New York
designers: Chris Riely, Jana Paterson
client: Tom Dolle Design

design firm: **Visual Asylum**
San Diego, California
designers: MaeLin Levine, Amy Jo Levine
client: Visual Asylum
(*Kuke Kristmas*)

design firm: **Visual Asylum**
San Diego, California
designers: MaeLin Levine, Amy Jo Levine
client: The Reserve Hotel Casino

170

design firm: **Oden Marketing & Design**
Memphis, Tennessee
design director:
Michael Guthrie
designers: Liz Allen, Michael Guthrie
creative director:
Bret Terwilleger
client: International Paper

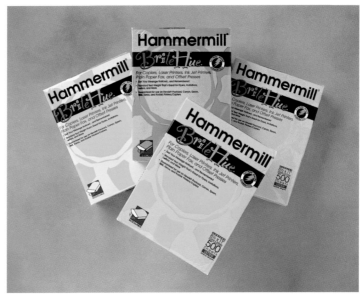

design firm: **Visual Asylum**
San Diego, California
designers: MaeLin Levine, Amy Jo Levine
client: Visual Asylum
(*A Real Nutcase*)

design firm: **Zebra Design**
Fairport, New York
designer: James L. Selak
client: Ice Communications

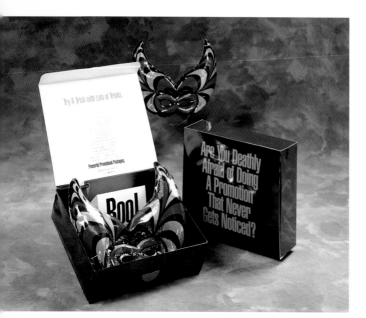

design firm: **H2D**
Milwaukee, Wisconsin
designer: Joe Hausch
client: PrismaGraphics

design firm: **Mires Design, Inc.**
San Diego, California
art director: José A. Serrano
designer: Miguel Perez
illustrator: Tracy Sabin
client: Bordeaux Printers

design firm: **Deskey Associates**
New York, New York
client: Day Timers, Inc.

design firm: **Mires Design, Inc.**
San Diego, California
art director: José A. Serrano
designers: José A. Serrano, Miguel Perez
illustrator: Tracy Sabin
client: Green Field Paper Company

design firm: **Visual Asylum**
San Diego, California
designers: MaeLin Levine, Amy Jo Levine,
Jason Janus
client: USD
(*Dr. Hughes Gift Book*)

design firm: **Kirima Design Office**
Osaka, Japan
designer: Harumi Kirima
client: Love Post Card Secretariat

design firm: **Adkins/Balchunas**
Providence, Rhode Island
designer: Jerry Balchunas
client: Big Noise

design firm: **M & Co.**
New York, New York
designers: Stefan Sagmeister, Tibor Kalman
photographer: Ed Lachman
client: Emi – Toshiba
(*YMO*)

design firm: **Sagmeister Inc.**
New York, New York
designers: Stefan Sagmeister,
Veronica Oh, Carola Pfeifer
client: Razor & Tie
(*The Nields*)

design firm: **Planet Design Co.**
              Madison, Wisconsin
designers: Planet Design Co.
client: Storm Music
              (*Alternative Pick*)

design firm: **Sayles Graphic Design**
              Des Moines, Iowa
designer: John Sayles
client: Flying Marsupials

175

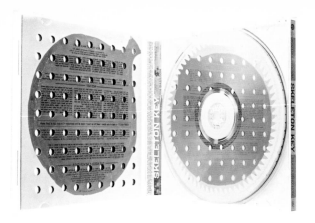

design firm: **Sagmeister Inc.**
New York, New York
designers: Stefan Sagmeister, Hjalti Karlsson
photographer: Tom Schierlitz
client: Capitol Records
(*Skeleton Key*)

design firm: **Sagmeister Inc.**
New York, New York
designers: Stefan Sagmeister, Hjalti Karlsson
illustrator: Hungry Dog Studios
client: Mahus Entertainment
(*Aerosmith*)

design firm: **Sagmeister Inc.**
New York, New York
designers: Stefan Sagmeister, Veronica Oh
illustrator: Eric Sanko
client: Motel Records
(*Skeleton Key*)

design firm: **Carbone Smolar Associates**
New York, New York
designers: John Nishimoto, Ken Carbone,
Karla Henrick
client: Nonesuch Records

177

design firm: **Adkins/Balchunas**
Providence, Rhode Island
designer: Jerry Balchunas
client: Flying Fish Records

design firm: **Sagmeister Inc.**
New York, New York
designers: Stefan Sagmeister, Veronica Oh
photographer: Jeffrey Silverthorne
client: Energy Records

design firm: **Sagmeister Inc.**
New York, New York
designers: Stefan Sagmeister, Veronica Oh
photographer: Tom Schierlitz
client: Razor & Tie
(*Marshall Crenshaw*)

design firm: **Segura Inc.**
             Chicago, Illinois
designer: Carlos Segura
client: TVT/ WaxTrax Records

design firm: **The Design Group**
New York, New York
designers: Stefan Sagmeister, Mike Chan
photographer: Bela Borsodi
client: Ubu Records
(*Songs of Maybe*)

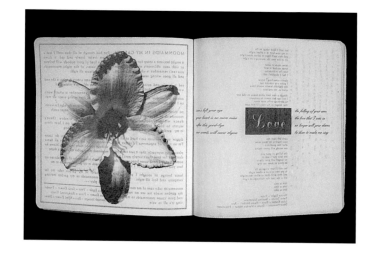

design firm: **Sibley Peteet Design**
Dallas, Texas
designer: Donna Aldridge
client: Jane Doe

design firm: **Sagmeister Inc.**
New York, New York
designers: Stefan Sagmeister,
Veronica Oh
photographer: Tom Schierlitz
client: Energy Records
(*H.P. Zinker*)

design firm: **Sagmeister Inc.**
New York, New York
designers: Stefan Sagmeister, Hjalti Karlsson
illustrators: Kevin Murphy, The Floating Company,
Gerard Howland
client: Promotone BV
(*The Rolling Stones*)

181

design firm: **Mires Design, Inc.**
                San Diego, California
art director: José A. Serrano
designer: Jeff Samaripa
photographer: David Deahl
client: Big Deahl

design firm: **Giles Design, Inc.**
                San Antonio, Texas
designers: Jill Giles, Warren Borror
client: Clampitt Paper Company

design firm: **Mires Design, Inc.**
                San Diego, California
art director: José A. Serrano
designer: Miguel Perez
photographer: Chris Wimpey
client: Deborah Liv Johnson